My World

MY BODY

By Gladys Rosa-Mendoza • Illustrations by Chris Butler

WINDMILL BOOKS
New York

Published in 2011 by Windmill Books, LLC
303 Park Avenue South, Suite # 1280, New York, NY 10010-3657

Adaptations to North American Edition © 2011 Windmill Books, LLC
First published by me+mi publishing, inc. © 2002
Text and illustrations copyright © me+mi publishing, inc., 2002

CREDITS:
Author: Gladys Rosa-Mendoza
Illustrator: Chris Butler

Library of Congress Cataloging-in-Publication Data

Rosa-Mendoza, Gladys.
 My body / by Gladys Rosa-Mendoza ; illustrated by Chris Butler. — School & Library ed.
     p. cm. — (My world)
 Originally published: Wheaton, IL : Me+mi Pub., 2002.
 Includes index.
 ISBN 978-1-60754-947-5 (library binding) — ISBN 978-1-61533-027-0 (pbk.) — ISBN 978-1-61533-028-7 (6 pack)
 1. Human body—Juvenile literature. I. Butler, Chris, ill. II. Title.
 QM27.R675 2010
 612—dc22
                          2009054402

Manufactured in the United States of America

For more great fiction and nonfiction, go to www.windmillbooks.com

CPSIA Compliance Information: Batch #S10W: For further information contact Windmill Books, New York, New York at 1-866-478-0556.

Contents

My name is Edward.

My name is Alicia.

Alicia has two brown eyes.

eyes

Edward has two ears. He points
to his nose.

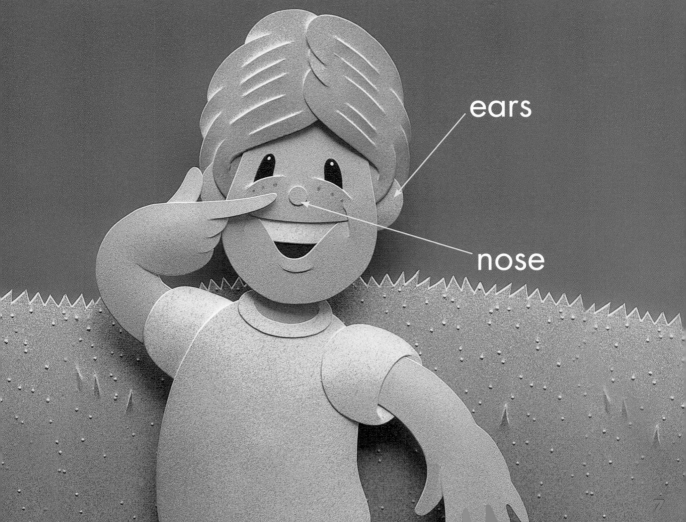

ears

nose

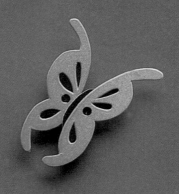

Alicia has two arms,
two hands, and two wrists.

hand

She waves at Edward.

wrist

arm

Edward has two elbows
and ten fingers.

elbow

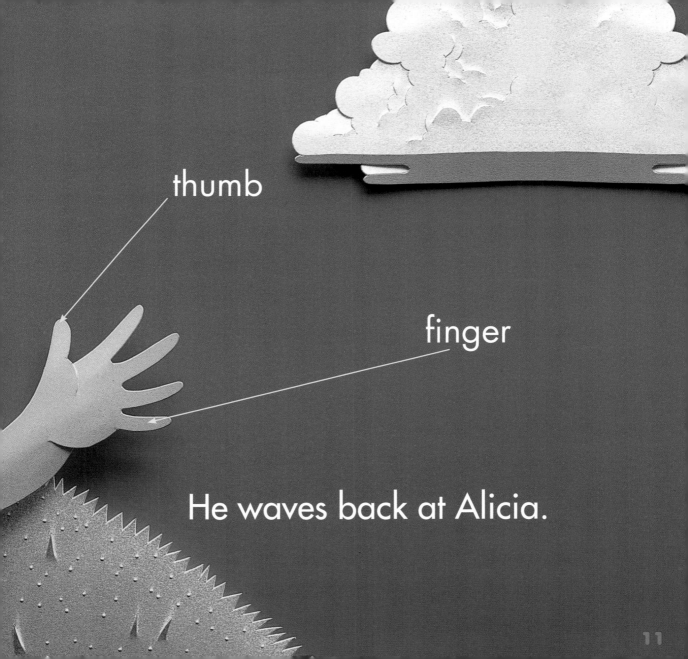

thumb

finger

He waves back at Alicia.

Alicia points to her mouth
and her teeth.

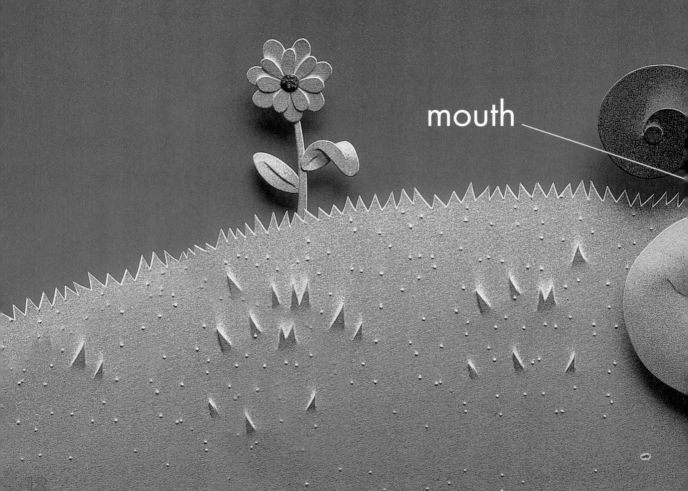

mouth

Edward has two legs,
two thighs, and two knees.

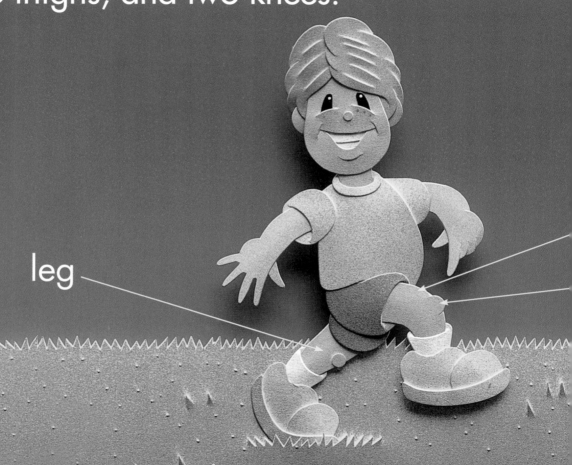

leg

He walks across the yard.

thigh

knee

Alicia has two feet, two ankles,

foot

toes

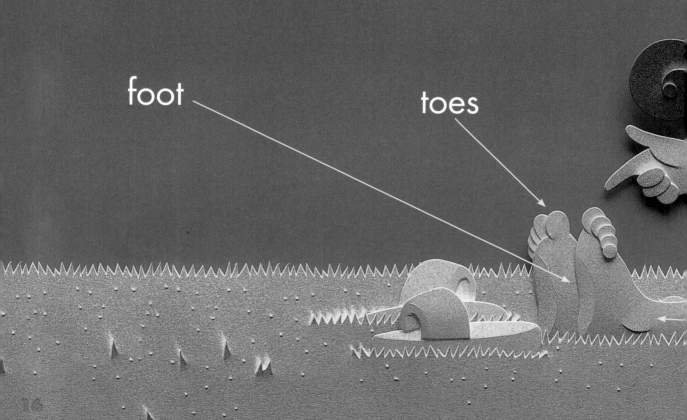

16

and ten toes.

She sits in the grass.

ankle

Alicia and Edward have many other parts, too.

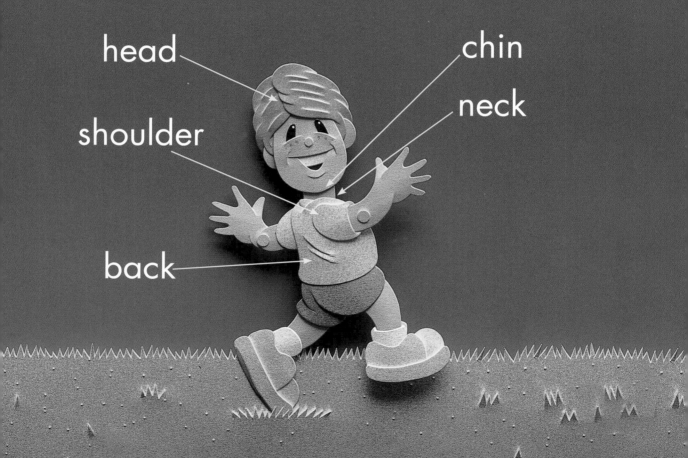

head

chin

neck

shoulder

back

Can you find these parts on your body?

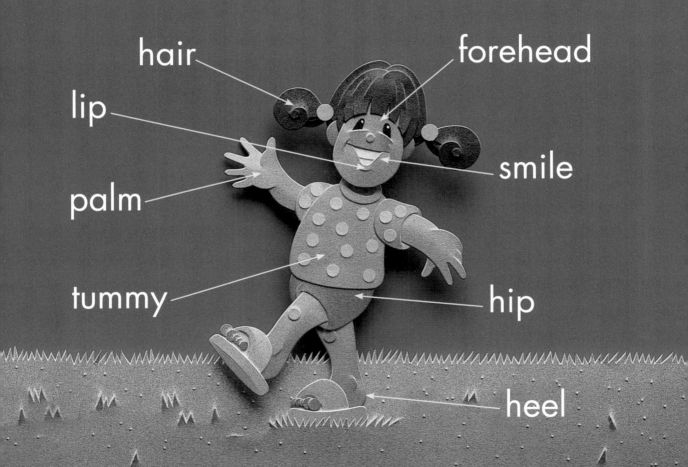

hair

forehead

lip

smile

palm

tummy

hip

heel

Read More!

Nonfiction

Manning, Mick. *Under Your Skin: Your Amazing Body.* Park Ridge, IL: Albert Whitman & Company, 2007.

Rabe, Tish. *Inside Your Outside: All About the Human Body.* New York: Random House, 2003.

Fiction

Arnold, Tedd. *More Parts.* New York: Puffin, 2003.

Schaefer, Lola. *Loose Tooth.* New York: HarperCollins, 2005.

Learn More!

 The longest bone in your body is in your thigh.

 The smallest bone in your body is in your ear.

 Your eyes are the same size as they were when you were born. Your nose and ears never stop growing.

How is your body different from when you were a baby? How is your body different from a monkey or a rabbit's body?

Words to Know

ankles (ANG-kulz) the joint between your leg and your foot

arm (AHRM) the limb that starts at your shoulder and ends at your hand

ears (EERZ) parts of your head that helps you to hear

elbows (EL-bohz) the joint in the middle of your arm that lets the arm bend

eyes (EYZ) the parts of your head that help you to see

feet (FEET) the parts of your body at the end of your legs that you walk on

22

hand (HAND) the part of your body at the end of your arm

mouth (MOWTH) the part of your head that lets you talk and eat

knee (NEE) the joint in the middle of your leg that lets the leg bend

nose (NOHZ) the part of your head that lets you smell

legs (LEGZ) the limbs that start at your hip and end at your feet

thumb (THUM) the short, thick first finger on your hand

23

Index

A
arm...8–9

E
ears...6–7
eyes...6

F
feet...16
fingers...10–11

H
hand...8–9

K
knees...15

L
legs...14

M
mouth...12

N
nose...7

T
toes...16–17

Web Sites

For Web resources related to the subject of this book, go to:
www.windmillbooks.com/weblinks and select this book's title